Holiday Art

Written by **Elizabeth McKinnon**

Illustrated by **Barb Tourtillotte**

Totline® Publications
A Division of Frank Schaffer Publications, Inc.
Torrance, California

Totline Publications would like to thank the following people for their contributions to this book: Ellen Bedford, Bridgeport, CT; Valerie Bielsker, Olathe, KS; Janice Bodenstedt, Jackson, MI; Barbara Fletcher, El Cajon, CA; Connie Gillilan, Hardy, NE; Janet Helgaas, Luverne, MN; Susan Olson Higgins, Shasta, CA; Barb Mazzochi, Glendale Heights, IL; Kathy McCullough, St. Charles, IL; Joleen Meier, Wausau, WI; Sharon L. Olson, Jamestown, ND; Natalie Page, Seattle, WA; Lois E. Putnam, Pilot Mountain, NC; Beverly Qualheim, Manitowoc, WI; Janet R. Reeves, Watertown, NY; Jane Roake, Oswego, IL; Barbara Robinson, Glendale, AZ; Betty Silkunas, New Wales, PA; Jacki Smallwood, Royersford, PA; Diane Thom, Maple Valley, WA; Elizabeth Vollrath, Stevens Point, WI; Nancy C. Windes, Denver, CO; Lamai Wyness, Danbury, CT.

Managing Editor: Mina McMullin
Contributing Editors: Durby Peterson, Jean Warren
Copyeditor: Kathy Zaun
Editorial Assistant: Mary Newmaster
Graphic Designer (Interior): Jill Kaufman
Graphic Designer (Cover): Brenda Mann Harrison
Illustrator (Cover): Barb Tourtillotte
Production Manager: Janie Schmidt

ISBN: 1-57029-282-5

Printed in the United States of America
Published by Totline® Publications
23740 Hawthorne Blvd.
Torrance, CA 90505

Introduction

At holiday times, young children enjoy exploring the colors and symbols of traditional celebrations through art projects.

In *Holiday Art,* you will find many ideas you can use to provide your children with creative hands-on experiences, ranging from open-ended holiday projects to easy holiday crafts. Each page contains a main activity plus a related activity for you to try with your group. All of the ideas are appropriate for young children and use materials that you are likely to have on hand.

Holiday Art includes activity suggestions for Halloween, Thanksgiving, Hanukkah, Christmas, Kwanzaa, Valentine's Day, St. Patrick's Day, and Easter. As you look through the book, you will see that some of the activities could be used for more than one holiday. For instance, the Hanukkah "Candle Creations" activity on page 28 could be adapted to make a Christmas or Kwanzaa gift. Or the "Christmas Tablecloth" activity on page 43 could be adapted to wrap up any of the holiday celebrations. Just let your imagination be your guide!

The activities in *Holiday Art* are designed to add to your seasonal art program. By using the ideas, you and your children are sure to experience many hours of creative fun. Happy holidays!

Contents

Halloween

Spooky Shapes

Cut large squares out of the financial pages or classified ads sections of old newspapers. Let your children choose squares and tear them into freeform shapes. Have them decorate their shapes with orange and black tempera paint. When the shapes have dried, mount them on a black paper background and display them on a wall or a bulletin board.

Quick Tip
Have your children practice tearing a few newspaper squares before they begin this activity, showing them how to start at one corner and continue tearing slowly.

Another Idea
Set out crayons or markers. Invite your children to use them to turn their shapes into "Halloween monsters."

Peekaboo Pumpkins

Set out orange tempera paint and paintbrushes and give each of your children two white paper plates. Have the children paint their plates orange on both the front and back sides. When the paint has dried, let them glue pumpkin seeds on the front sides of both plates. Then staple each child's plates together, front sides facing, to make a "pumpkin," leaving a small opening at the top for the child to peek through to see the seeds. For a finishing touch, give the children green construction-paper stems to glue to the tops of their pumpkins.

Quick Tip
This activity provides a great way to use the seeds from a carved jack-o'-lantern.

☀ Another Idea
Give each of your children two identical pumpkin shapes cut from orange construction paper and stapled together on the left-hand side, like a book. Have the children draw faces on the outside of their pumpkins and glue pumpkin seeds inside.

Jack-O'-Lantern Faces

Give each of your children a large pumpkin shape cut out of orange construction paper. Set out various sizes of triangles and circles cut from black construction paper for the children to use to make faces on their pumpkins. Encourage them to arrange the shapes in various ways on their pumpkins until they are satisfied with the faces. Then have them glue the shapes in place.

☀ Another Idea
Let your children print faces on their pumpkins using small sponge triangles dipped into black tempera paint.

Halloween Spider Webs

Pour black tempera paint into a small bowl and add one or two marbles. Let each of your children place a small paper plate in a pie tin or a similar container. Spoon in the paint-covered marbles and have the child tilt the pie tin, rolling the marbles back and forth to create a black "spider web" on the paper plate. Allow the paint to dry. Then let the children glue one or more small black pompoms onto their webs for spiders.

Another Idea

For each of your children, cut slits around the edges of a small, sturdy paper plate, and tape a long piece of black yarn to the front. Let your children make webs by weaving the yarn back and forth across the back of their plates, passing it through the slits any way they wish. Have them glue black button "spiders" onto their webs.

Bouncing Bats

For each of your children, cut out two adjoining egg cups, in one piece, from a cardboard egg carton (one egg carton will provide six bats). Give the egg cup sections to the children to use for making bat bodies. Help them turn their egg cup sections upside down and trim the edges, if necessary. Then have them paint their sections inside and out with black tempera paint to make "bats." When the paint has dried, let them attach small yellow circle stickers for eyes. Poke a hole in the top of each child's bat and thread a knotted rubber band through it for a hanger. Show the children how to hold onto the hangers and bounce their bats up and down.

Quick Tip

If you have a large group, ask parents to donate empty cardboard egg cartons to use for this activity.

Another Idea

Invite your children to make fingerpaintings with black paint. When dry, cut the papers into bat shapes and display them on a wall or a bulletin board.

Trick-or-Treat Art

For each of your children, cut a large house shape out of black construction paper. From magazines and store flyers, cut out pictures of children in Halloween costumes. Let your children use white chalk to draw windows and a door on their house shapes. Then invite them to choose one or two pictures of children in costumes to glue onto their houses for trick-or-treaters. When they have finished, display their decorated houses on a wall or bulletin board to create a "Halloween neighborhood."

Another Idea

Give your children brown paper grocery bags with handles. Set out pictures of Halloween symbols, candy, and costumes cut from magazines, newspapers, and store flyers. Invite the children to glue the pictures onto their paper bags to make Halloween treat bags.

Shape Masks

From various colors of construction paper, cut out large shapes, such as circles, rectangles, or ovals. Cut two eye holes in each shape. Set out glue along with collage materials, such as paper and fabric scraps, yarn pieces, ribbons, and stickers. Let each of your children choose a shape and decorate it with the collage materials to make a mask, adding details with crayons or markers. Encourage the children to think about what the shapes suggest. For instance, an oval might be turned into a fish mask, or a square might make a robot face. When the children have finished, glue or tape a craft-stick handle to the back of each mask so that it can be held in front of the child's face.

Quick Tip
These masks do not restrict seeing, making them perfect for young children.

Another Idea
When your children have completed their masks, let them use crayons or markers to decorate construction paper headbands. Then attach each child's mask to his or her headband so that the mask stands above the child's forehead. Fasten the ends of the headband in place with tape.

Halloween Streamers

Help your children trace around pumpkin cookie cutters on orange construction paper and cut out the shapes. Set out black crayons or markers and have the children decorate their pumpkins with jack-o'-lantern faces. Encourage them to make as many decorated pumpkins as they wish. When they have finished, glue the pumpkins, one beneath the other, on black crepe-paper streamers. Use the streamers as wall decorations. Or, hang them in a doorway so the children can walk through them as they enter or leave the room.

 Another Idea

Use white adding machine paper to make streamers. Let your children decorate the streamers with orange and black marker designs and Halloween stickers or rubber-stamp prints.

Thanksgiving

Harvest Veggie Prints

Cut large brown paper grocery bags into cornucopia shapes. Select a variety of vegetables, such as potatoes, carrots, turnips, cauliflower florets, or mushrooms, and cut each one in half. Make paint pads by placing folded paper towels in shallow containers and pouring on small amounts of tempera paint in autumn colors. Invite your children to press the cut sides of the vegetables onto the paint pads, then onto their cornucopias to make Harvest Veggie Prints.

Another Idea

Set out white paper plates. Let your children print on them with the vegetables to create harvest "dinners."

Cornmeal Dough Fun

Make Cornmeal Dough following the recipe below. Give your children pieces of the dough to roll, poke, and pound as they wish. Then have them flatten their dough pieces into circles or ovals. Set out a variety of dried beans for them to press into their dough circles to make Thanksgiving plaques. Allow the plaques to dry for several days until they are hard.

 Another Idea

Take your children on a walk to collect small, fresh leaves, flat twigs, and pebbles. Let them use their nature finds instead of dried beans to decorate their Cornmeal Dough circles.

Cornmeal Dough

1 cup water

1 cup salt

1 ½ cups flour

1 ½ cups yellow cornmeal

Combine all the ingredients in a large bowl and knead well. Add a tiny bit more water or flour, if needed. Store leftover dough in the refrigerator in an airtight container.

Feathery Turkeys

For each of your children, cut a large turkey shape out of brown construction paper. Pour glue into shallow containers. Provide brushes and set out feathers in a variety of colors. Invite the children to brush the glue onto their turkey shapes and place the feathers on top of the glue.

Quick Tip
Colorful feathers to use for art activities can be found at arts and crafts stores.

Another Idea
Have your children tear scraps of red, yellow, and orange construction paper into small pieces and glue them onto their turkey shapes for feathers.

Little Hand Turkeys

Cut brown paper grocery bags into large squares. Help your children trace around their hands on the squares and cut out the shapes to use for making "turkeys." Using crayons, have them color the palm of each hand shape brown for a turkey body, the fingers orange and yellow for feathers, and the thumb red for a turkey head. Help them glue or tape their turkeys to pieces of construction paper. Then have them use crayons to add details to each turkey, such as an eye, a beak, a wattle, and legs.

Another Idea

Draw a large barnyard scene on a piece of butcher paper. Help your children attach their Little Hand Turkeys to the paper and add details, as suggested in the main activity, to make a Thanksgiving mural.

Fragrant Holiday Pies

Give each of your children a large circle cut from orange construction paper. Pour glue into shallow containers and provide brushes. Set out powdered cinnamon and ginger in shaker containers and place several whole cloves in a small paper cup for each child. Invite the children to brush glue all over their papers. Then have them sprinkle on the cinnamon, ginger, and cloves to make "pumpkin pies" that smell mm-mmm good!

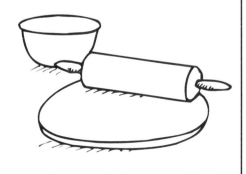

Another Idea

Use a favorite recipe to make modeling dough and add ground cinnamon instead of food coloring. Let your children use the dough with baking toys, such as small pans, rolling pins, and plastic knives, to make pretend pies.

Thanksgiving Placemats

Select a piece of construction paper for each of your children. Write "I Am Thankful" around the edges of each paper to form a border. Have your children look through magazines and tear or cut out pictures of things they are thankful for. Let them glue the pictures onto their papers, inside the borders, to make Thanksgiving Placemats. Cover the papers with clear self-stick paper for durability, if you wish.

Quick Tip

These placemats can be used at snacktime or taken home to use as decorations for the Thanksgiving table.

Another Idea

Let your children make placemats by decorating pieces of construction paper with Thanksgiving stickers and crayon or marker designs.

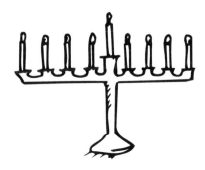

Hanukkah

Star of David Prints

Find a Star of David cookie cutter. Using a marker, trace around the cookie cutter on a thin, flat sponge and cut out the shape with scissors. Continue in the same way to make several stars. Pour several colors of tempera paint into shallow containers. Have your children dip the sponge stars into the paints and use them to make prints on pieces of white construction paper or butcher paper. When the paint has dried, let the children use the paper to make Hanukkah cards or to wrap gifts.

Quick Tip

If you don't have a Star of David cookie cutter, you can make a cardboard pattern. Just draw one triangle upside down on top of an identical triangle, as shown, and cut out the six-pointed star.

Another Idea

Have your children print stars on lunch bags to use for gift bags. Invite them to add sparkly designs with glitter-glue pens.

Decorated Dreidels

For each of your children, tape a large piece of heavy-duty foil to the top of your art table. Pour white glue into small containers and add drops of food coloring to each one. Invite your children to dip cotton swabs into the colored glue and use them like brushes to paint designs on their foil pieces. Allow the glue to dry overnight. Then cut the foil pieces into dreidel shapes and mount them on construction paper to display as holiday decorations.

Another Idea

Cut dreidel shapes out of construction paper. Have your children decorate them by brushing on glue that has been mixed with glitter.

Candle Creations

Invite your children to make candles by painting 4½-inch cardboard tubes blue. When the paint has dried, have the children glue their candles upright onto 5- to 6-inch circles that have been cut from white posterboard. Set out gold glitter-glue pens for the children to use to decorate their candles and posterboard-circle candle bases. For a finishing touch, help them brush a little glue around the inside tops of their candles. Then show them how to make a flame by pinching the center of a 5-inch yellow tissue-paper square and poking the square down into the glue on the top inside of the candle, as shown in the illustration.

Quick Tip
These Candle Creations make nice holiday gifts.

Another Idea

Have your children turn baby food jars into candleholders by gluing on torn pieces of blue and white tissue paper. Help them tie gold cord around the rims of their jars and insert holiday votive candles.

Menorah Pictures

For each of your children, use a crayon or a marker to draw a simple menorah, as shown in the illustration, on a piece of construction paper. Set out glue and give each child nine birthday candles with the wicks trimmed off. Invite the children to glue the candles onto their menorah pictures. Then give them each nine candle-flame shapes cut from yellow construction paper to glue above their candles.

Another Idea

Let your children glue plastic straw segments onto their menorah pictures for candles and add yellow fingerprints for flames.

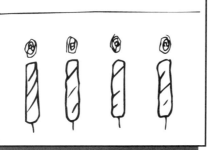

Christmas

Shiny Foil Art

For each of your children, tear off a piece of heavy-duty aluminum foil and wrap the edges around a square of cardboard. Invite the children to tear assorted colors of tissue paper into small scraps. Have them brush glue onto their foil pieces. Then have them arrange the tissue scraps on top of the glue, leaving spaces for the foil to shine through and create a mirror effect. When the glue has dried, tape a construction paper frame around each child's decorated foil piece.

Quick Tip
Shiny Foil Art makes nice wrapping paper for small gifts.

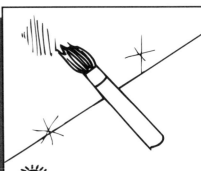

Another Idea
Let your children paint designs on sheets of aluminum foil using tempera paint mixed with drops of liquid dishwashing detergent.

Evergreen Art

Cut evergreen branches into sprigs about 3- or 4-inches long. Pour green tempera paint in shallow containers and set out pieces of white construction paper. Let your children choose evergreen sprigs and use them to brush the paint in designs on their papers. When they have finished, help them tape or staple their sprigs to their decorated papers, if they wish.

Quick Tip

Check a Christmas tree lot for leftover branches to cut into sprigs. Try for a variety of evergreens, if available.

 Another Idea

Cut Christmas tree shapes out of light green construction paper. Let your children use evergreen sprigs to brush designs onto the tree shapes with dark green tempera paint.

Handy Christmas Trees

Spread thick green tempera paint in the bottom of a shallow container and set out pieces of light-colored construction paper. Help each of your children in turn make a Handy Christmas Tree, following these directions: Have the child place a hand in the paint and make three prints on the paper, two near the bottom facing right and left for the lower branches of the tree, and one facing straight up to represent the top branches. (Have the child dip his or her hand into the paint before making each of the prints.) Allow the paint to dry. Then show the children how to dip a finger into red tempera paint and decorate their trees with fingerprint "Christmas balls" all over the branches. They can dip a finger in yellow tempera paint to add a fingerprint "star" to the top of the tree.

☀ Another Idea

Help each child trace around his or her hand on green construction paper three times and cut out the shapes. Have the children glue their shapes onto light-colored paper to make trees like those described in the main activity. Let them add holiday stickers for decorations.

Salt Glitter Trees

Make trees by cutting large triangles out of green construction paper or posterboard. Set out glue and several colors of Salt Glitter (see recipe below), along with a shallow box or pan for each color. Have each of your children in turn place a tree shape in a box and dribble on glue designs. Help the child sprinkle on one color of Salt Glitter and tap the excess salt back into the box. Then let the child dribble on more glue designs and sprinkle on another color of salt. Continue in the same manner until the tree is decorated to the child's liking.

Another Idea

Let your children decorate their trees by gluing on a combination of Salt Glitter and small circles punched out of colorful construction paper.

Salt Glitter

food coloring

salt

To make each color, stir 5 or 6 drops of food coloring into ½ cup salt and mix well. Spread out the salt on waxed paper to dry, or microwave it for 1 to 2 minutes. Pour the colored salt into shaker containers.

Stencil Christmas Cards

Use plastic-foam plates to make stencils. Press Christmas cookie cutters into the bottom of the plates. Cut out the shapes in one piece with a craft knife (save the shapes to use for the activity in Another Idea, if you wish). Help your children fold pieces of light-colored construction paper in half to make blank cards. Then show them how to place the stencils on top of the front of their cards and use crayons or markers to fill in the center of the stencils. Write dictated holiday greetings inside the cards and help the children sign their names.

Another Idea

Have your children place Christmas shapes cut from plastic-foam plates on pieces of bright-colored construction paper. Let them spatter-paint over the shapes by dipping toothbrushes into white tempera paint and rubbing across the brushes with craft sticks. Allow the paint to dry before removing the shapes. Use the decorated papers to make cards.

Holiday Wreaths

Cut the centers out of enough paper plates to give a rim to each of your children. Have them cut or tear old Christmas cards and gift-wrap scraps into small pieces. Set out the pieces along with other Christmas collage materials, such as holiday stickers, used gift tags, ribbon, and tinsel. Invite the children to make wreaths by gluing the collage materials onto their plate rims, covering them completely. For a finishing touch, give them self-stick bows to attach to the tops of their wreaths.

Quick Tip

Ask parents to donate used or leftover Christmas decorating materials for this activity.

Another Idea

Set out green ink pads and an assortment of rubber stamps. Let your children stamp green prints all over their plate rims to make wreaths. Then have them attach colorful self-stick bows.

Rudolph Reindeers

Give each of your children a 9-inch triangle cut from brown construction paper to use for making a reindeer face. Have the children place their triangles on a table with one point facing down, and fold over the two top corners to make ears. Let them glue on black construction-paper circles for eyes and a red circle for a nose. Then give them twigs to tape to the tops of their triangles for antlers. Display the Rudolph Reindeers around your room as holiday decorations.

💡 **Another Idea**

Help your children make antlers for their reindeer by tracing around their hands on yellow construction paper, cutting out the shapes, and taping the shapes to the tops of their Rudolph faces.

Christmas Stockings

For each of your children, put together two pieces of construction paper and cut them into a large stocking shape. With the two shapes together, use a hole punch to make holes around the sides and bottom of each stocking shape. Let your children decorate their stocking shapes with crayon or marker designs and holiday stickers. Then have them use long pieces of yarn (tape one end of each piece) to lace their stocking shapes together, leaving the tops open. When they have finished, tie a loop of yarn to each Christmas Stocking and hang them around the room.

 Another Idea

Make a stocking for each of your children by folding a piece of construction paper in half lengthwise and cutting out a stocking shape, so that the fold forms the back of the stocking. Invite the children to open their stockings and glue on pictures of toys cut or torn from holiday ads or catalogs.

Spicy Ornaments

Give each of your children a small amount of Cinnamon Dough (see recipe below). Have them flatten it to about ¼-inch thick on a lightly floured surface. Have the children use cookie cutters to cut Christmas shapes out of the dough. Help them use a plastic straw to poke a hole in the top of each shape. Allow the shapes to air dry for at least 48 hours, turning them over every now and then to make sure that they remain flat. When the Spicy Ornaments are completely dry, thread loops of red yarn or ribbon through the holes for hangers.

 Another Idea

Let your children make scented ornaments by brushing glue onto plastic-foam Christmas shapes and sprinkling on powdered red or green gelatin. Add a yarn or ribbon hanger to each ornament.

Cinnamon Dough

ground cinnamon

applesauce (ordinary variety, not chunky)

all-purpose white glue

In a large bowl, combine four parts cinnamon, three parts applesauce, and one part glue. Knead until well blended. (A mixture of 4 tablespoons cinnamon, 3 tablespoons applesauce, and 1 tablespoon glue will be enough for about three small ornaments.)

Gingerbag Houses

For each of your children, wash and dry a half-pint milk carton to use for making a "house." From a brown paper grocery bag, cut a strip to fit around and cover all four sides of the carton. Glue it in place. Staple the top of the carton closed. Then glue or staple a piece of folded brown paper over the top of the carton for a roof. Set out glue and collage materials, such as construction paper and fabric scraps, white reinforcement circles, stickers, yarn, ribbon, rickrack, beads, buttons, tinsel, and sequins. Then invite the children to decorate their houses by gluing on the materials any way they wish, helping them to add doors, windows, and other features as desired.

Quick Tip

Provide your children with design ideas for this activity by displaying pictures of decorated gingerbread houses found in holiday books and magazines.

Another Idea

Cover individual cereal boxes with brown paper for your children to decorate as stores and other buildings. Arrange the decorated houses and buildings together to create a holiday village.

Festive Banners

Give each of your children a 9-inch square of felt plus a Christmas tree shape cut from green felt to fit on the square. Cut colored felt scraps into small pieces. Help the children glue their tree shapes onto their felt squares. Then invite them to decorate their trees by gluing on the colored felt pieces. Turn the squares into banners by gluing loops of felt to the top of each square for hangers. When the glue has dried, insert dowels or thin branches through the hangers and display the banners around your room.

Quick Tip
Festive Banners make nice holiday gifts that are sure to be treasured year after year.

Another Idea
Have your children glue other felt Christmas shapes, such as stars or bells, onto their felt squares. Let them decorate the shapes with small felt pieces and add sparkly designs with glitter-glue pens.

Christmas Tablecloth

Cover your work area with white butcher paper and place a plain white paper tablecloth on top of it. Set out washable red and green ink pads along with large rubber stamps in Christmas or seasonal shapes. Invite your children to make a festive covering for your snack table by using the materials to stamp prints all over the tablecloth.

Quick Tip

You might want to save your children's Christmas Tablecloth for a one-time celebration, since spills may cause the colors to run.

Another Idea

Make a tablecloth out of butcher paper. Cover the tablecloth with Christmas shapes—stars, reindeer, Santas, and so forth—by tracing around cookie cutters. Let your children color the shapes and add designs with crayons or markers.

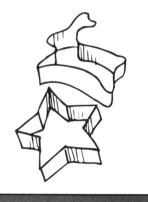

Kwanzaa

Fruit Collages

Give each of your children a paper plate. Set out brushes and glue in shallow containers. Invite the children to look through magazines, supermarket ads, and seed catalogs to find pictures of different kinds of fruit. Have them cut or tear out the pictures and glue them all over their paper plates to create Fruit Collages.

 Another Idea

Cut fruit, such as apples, oranges, or lemons, in half. Let your children dip the cut edges of the fruit into tempera paint and press them onto white construction paper to make prints.

Corncob Printing

Save cobs from a corn-on-the-cob meal and allow them to dry for several days. Place folded paper towels in shallow containers and pour on small amounts of tempera paint. If available, stick holders into the ends of the dried corncobs. Let your children roll the cobs onto the paint pads, then onto pieces of construction paper or butcher paper to make prints.

Quick Tip
Let your children use their corncob-printed papers to make Kwanzaa cards or to wrap gifts.

Another Idea
Break or cut the corncobs into sections. Invite your children to use the ends of the cob sections to print designs on paper.

Kwanzaa Necklaces

Give each of your children several African animal shapes, each about 2½ inches long, cut from yellow construction paper. Have the children use markers to draw eyes and other details on both sides of their shapes. Using a hole punch, make a hole in the center of each shape. Let the children string large pieces of pasta, such as rigatoni, onto 2-foot-long yarn pieces with their animal shapes in between. When they have finished, tie each child's yarn ends together to make a necklace.

Quick Tip
These handmade necklaces make nice Kwanzaa gifts.

Another Idea
Have your children color pieces of stringable pasta with red, green, and black tempera paint. Let them make necklaces by threading the pasta onto yarn pieces.

Kwanzaa Placemats

Give each of your children a piece of white construction paper. Set out washable red, green, and black ink pads. For each color, provide an assortment of rubber stamps of any kind. Invite your children to choose stamps and print red, green, and black designs all over their papers to make placemats. When the ink has dried, cover the placemats with clear self-stick paper for durability, if you wish.

 Another Idea

Make groups of red, green, and black crayons, with the points even, and fasten each group together with masking tape. Invite your children to make placemats by using the crayons to draw arcs, wavy lines, and other designs on their papers.

Valentine's Day

Shiny Hearts

Cut large heart shapes out of white posterboard. For each of your children, mix about 2 tablespoons of light corn syrup with a squirt of liquid dishwashing detergent in a small cup. Tint the mixture with red food coloring. Set out brushes or cotton swabs, and give each child a heart shape. Invite the children to paint designs on their hearts with the colored corn-syrup mixture. Allow several days for the designs to dry before displaying the Shiny Hearts as valentine decorations.

Another Idea
Add sparkle to the hearts by stirring a small amount of silver glitter into the colored corn-syrup mixture.

Heart Wreaths

For each of your children, cut an 8- to 9-inch ring out of cardboard or posterboard. Set out an assortment of materials, such as construction paper, gift-wrap, aluminum foil, computer paper, newspaper comics, advertisements, and colorful magazine pages. Help your children trace around heart cookie cutters on the various materials and cut out the shapes. Then have them glue their hearts onto their cardboard rings, covering the rings completely, to make Heart Wreaths. Poke a hole in the top of each wreath and tie on a loop of yarn or ribbon for a hanger.

Another Idea

Cut the centers out of paper plates. Let your children make wreaths by gluing small valentines onto the plate rims.

Marbleized Hearts

Cut 3- to 4-inch heart shapes out of white construction paper. Make Marbleizing Mixture (see recipe below) and place it on top of old newspapers with paper towels spread out nearby. Help each of your children in turn dip one (or more) heart into the mixture and immediately place it on the paper towels. Add more drops of food coloring as needed. When the hearts have dried, hang them in a window as translucent valentine decorations.

Another Idea
Have your children glue their Marbleized Hearts onto folded pieces of red construction paper to make valentine cards.

Marbleizing Mixture

1 cup hot water

1 Tbsp. white vinegar

1 Tbsp. vegetable oil

red food coloring

In a shallow pan, combine water, vinegar, and oil. Add drops of food coloring and swirl them around.

Heart Cutups

Set out a piece of red construction paper for each of your children. Fold pieces of white and pink paper in half and cut them into heart shapes. Then cut heart-shaped centers out of the hearts, as shown. (Let older children cut out the heart centers by themselves, if they wish.) Set out all the hearts and shallow containers of glue. Have the children brush the glue onto their red construction papers and arrange the Heart Cutups on top of the glue any way they wish.

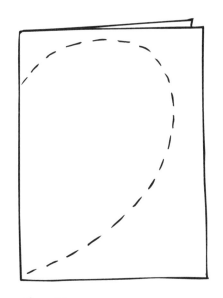
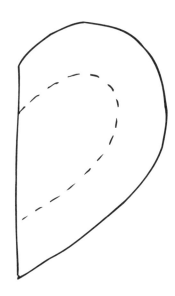

Another Idea

Give your children folded heart shapes and let them snip out freeform shapes along the folds, as if cutting snowflake designs. Have them open their unique hearts and glue them onto their papers.

Loving Hands Valentines

Help each of your children, one at a time, coat the palms and fingers of both hands with red paint. Show each child how to make his or her handprints form the shape of a heart on the center of a paper doily by following these steps: With fingers together, press one hand onto the doily to make a print. Then with the other hand, also with fingers together, press so that the palms form the upper part of the heart and the fingers turn inward and overlap to form the point at the bottom of the heart. When the paint has dried, glue each doily onto red construction paper and write "I'm handing you my heart on Valentine's Day!" plus the child's name at the bottom of the paper.

Another Idea

Help your children trace around one of their hands on red construction paper and cut out the shapes. Have them glue their hand shapes onto small doilies and then glue the doilies to pieces of pink construction paper. On each paper, write "A Handful of Love" plus the child's name.

Old-Fashioned Valentines

Make blank cards by folding pieces of red, pink, or white construction paper in half. Set out red, pink, or white collage materials, such as paper heart shapes, valentine stickers, paper doilies, yarn, ribbon, rickrack, and glitter glue. Invite your children to choose blank cards and glue the collage materials onto the fronts to create Old-Fashioned Valentines. When they have finished, write dictated messages inside the cards and help them sign their names.

Quick Tip

Inspire your children by displaying examples of traditional lacy valentines.

Another Idea

Cut large heart shapes out of red posterboard or construction paper and write "Happy Valentine's Day" on each one. Let your children decorate the hearts with collage materials to make valentines.

Doily Decorations

From red and pink paper, such as construction paper or gift-wrap, cut out small heart shapes. Let your children help you use a hole punch to punch small circles out of the red and pink paper scraps. Cut paper lace into small pieces. Set out the hearts, small circles, and paper lace pieces and give each child a paper doily. Invite the children to decorate their doilies by brushing on glue and arranging the hearts, circles, and lace pieces on top of the glue. When the glue has dried, attach a loop of red or pink yarn to the top of each doily. Then hang the Doily Decorations around the room.

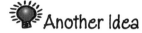

Another Idea

Let your children decorate paper hearts as desired and glue them onto small doilies. Arrange the doilies around the edge of a bulletin board as a valentine border.

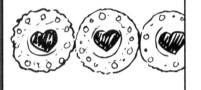

Valentine Bags

For each of your children, select a paper lunch bag to use for making a "love bug" Valentine Bag. Using scissors, round off the top of each bag, then fold down the top to create a blank "face," with the rounded part forming the chin. Set out assorted sizes of heart shapes cut from red construction paper. Let your children make ears by gluing hearts to the back of their bags, near the top, as shown. Then let them glue on additional hearts to create faces. Have them use more hearts or markers to add other details, if they wish. Encourage the children to use their bags for holding valentines or other holiday goodies.

Quick Tip

If available, white paper lunch bags would work well for this activity.

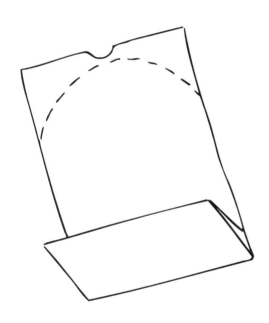

Another Idea

Have your children decorate plain bags by rubber-stamping heart prints all over the sides or by attaching valentine stickers.

St. Patrick's Day

Shamrock Collages

For each of your children, cut a large shamrock shape out of green construction paper or posterboard. Set out green collage materials, such as paper and fabric scraps, yarn, ribbon, rickrack, stickers, pasta shapes, Easter grass, twist ties, and confetti. Invite your children to brush glue all over their shamrock shapes and arrange the collage materials on top of the glue.

💡 **Another Idea**

Have your children look through magazines and catalogs to find green pictures. Let them cut or tear out the pictures and glue them onto their shamrock shapes.

Shamrock Prints

Collect small aluminum cans for making jumbo shamrock stamps. To make each stamp, use strapping tape or duct tape to fasten three cans together in a shamrock shape. Place folded paper towels in shallow containers and pour on small amounts of green tempera paint to make paint pads. Set out pieces of white construction paper. Let your children press the shamrock stamps onto the paint pads, then onto their papers to make prints. Have them use paint or markers to add stems to their shamrocks.

 Another Idea
Set out white paper and washable green ink pads. Show your children how to make groups of three fingerprints on their papers to create shamrocks. Invite them to add crayon or marker stems.

Colorful Rainbows

Give each of your children a piece of white construction paper and several different colors of tissue paper. Pour liquid starch into shallow containers and set out brushes. Have the children tear their tissue paper into small pieces, keeping each color in a separate pile. Help the children brush an arc of liquid starch on their papers. Show them how to cover the arc with tissue pieces of one color. When they have completed one arc, have them make other colored arcs under the first one. Allow the starch to dry. Then display the Colorful Rainbows on a wall or a bulletin board.

Quick Tip

If you want to use real rainbow colors for this activity, they are red, orange, yellow, green, blue, and purple.

Another Idea

Have your children make long paper chains, each in a different color. Attach the chains to a wall or a bulletin board in arcs, one under the other, to make a giant rainbow for your room. Add a paper "pot of gold" to one end of the rainbow, if you wish.

Leprechaun Puppets

Give each of your children a 3- to 4-inch circle cut from white construction paper. Have the children draw on a leprechaun face with crayons or markers, and glue on a fluffed-out cotton ball for a beard. Provide strips of green construction paper, about 1 by 4½ inches. Show the children how to accordion-fold the strips and glue or tape them to their leprechaun faces for arms and legs. Give them black hat shapes to glue onto their leprechauns and a St. Patrick's Day sticker to attach for a hat decoration. To complete the Leprechaun Puppets, glue or tape a craft stick to the back of each one for a handle.

Another Idea

Let your children draw leprechaun faces on small paper plates. Have them glue on pieces of orange or red yarn for beards and hair, and add green hat shapes cut from construction paper. When they have finished, attach a craft-stick handle to the back of each puppet.

St. Patrick's Day Hats

For each of your children, cut six 4-inch shamrock shapes out of green construction paper. Make a headband for each child by taping together, end to end, two 1-by-12-inch strips of white construction paper, trimming the band to fit around the child's forehead, and taping the ends closed. Have the children remove their headbands and glue on five of their shamrock shapes. Staple each child's sixth shamrock shape to the top of a piece of green pipe cleaner that is about 6 inches long. Staple the other end of the pipe cleaner to the front of the child's headband so that it stands straight up from the band. After covering the staples with tape, help the children put on their completed St. Patrick's Day Hats.

Quick Tip
Trace around a shamrock cookie cutter to make a shamrock pattern for this activity.

Another Idea
Let your children decorate sheets of white construction paper with green crayon or marker designs and St. Patrick's Day stickers. Then roll each paper into a cone shape and tape the edges together to make a hat for each child.

St. Patrick's Day Streamers

Cut green crepe-paper streamers into long pieces. Set out washable dark green ink pads and rubber stamps in shamrock shapes. Invite your children to use the ink pads and rubber stamps to print shamrocks all over the streamers. When the ink has dried, hang the streamers around your room for St. Patrick's Day decorations.

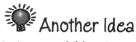

Another Idea

Invite your children to decorate green construction-paper shamrock shapes with green glitter-glue designs. Then glue the shamrocks onto white crepe-paper streamers.

Easter

Glossy-Colored Eggs

Pour sweetened, condensed milk into small containers and add drops of different-colored food coloring to each one. Cut large egg shapes out of white posterboard. Invite your children to paint bands of the brightly colored milk across their egg shapes, covering them completely. When they have finished, place their Glossy-Colored Eggs on paper towels and allow them to dry for several days.

 Another Idea

For a softer effect, have your children paint their egg shapes with evaporated milk that has been tinted with drops of food coloring.

Blended-Color Eggs

Cut egg shapes out of white construction paper. Set out assorted colors of washable markers and pour water into small containers. Show your children how to use the markers to draw bands of different colors on their egg shapes. Then have them paint water over their eggs and watch as the colors run and blend together. When the egg shapes have dried, use them as Easter decorations.

💡 **Another Idea**

Let your children use various colors of chalk to draw designs on their egg shapes. Then show them how to blend the colors by rubbing across the shapes with facial tissue.

Eggshell Art

Save the shells from hard-boiled eggs. Wash and dry the eggshells, then gently break them into small pieces. From posterboard, cut out Easter shapes, such as bunnies, eggs, or chicks. Have your children brush glue all over the shapes and sprinkle the eggshell pieces on top of the glue. When the glue has dried, let the children paint over the eggshell-covered shapes using pastel colors of tempera paint.

Quick Tip

Ask parents to save eggshells for you to use for this activity. Make sure that the shells are from eggs that have been hard-boiled.

 Another Idea

Dye eggshell pieces in containers of diluted food coloring and spread them out to dry on paper towels. Let your children make collages by gluing the colored eggshell pieces onto pieces of construction paper.

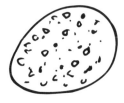

Easter Cards

Make a blank card for each of your children by folding a piece of white construction paper in half. Show the children how to open their cards and use crayons or markers to draw designs all over the right-hand side. When they have finished, cut a large egg shape out of the front of each card so that the designs inside show through the shape. Write "Happy Easter" on the front of each card and help the children sign their names inside.

Quick Tip

For easy cutting, first draw or trace an egg shape on the front of a card. Then with a craft knife, cut a large X in the center of the shape to allow access for your scissors.

Another Idea

Invite your children to decorate the insides of their cards by gluing on small squares of brightly colored tissue paper.

Fluffy Bunnies

Cut bunny shapes, as shown in the illustration, out of white construction paper. Set out brushes and shallow containers of glue. Provide cotton balls and show your children how to gently fluff them out. Give the bunny shapes to the children. Have them brush glue all over their shapes and arrange the cotton on top of the glue. For a final touch, let each child glue one round cotton ball onto his or her Fluffy Bunny for a tail.

 Another Idea

Have your children make Easter pictures by gluing their Fluffy Bunnies onto pieces of light blue construction paper. Let them add a little Easter grass plus a few Easter egg stickers.

Bunny Puppets

Cut white paper plates in half. Give each of your children one of the plate halves to use for a bunny body. Have the children place their plates with the curved edge at the top to represent the bunny's back. Let them glue a cotton ball at one end of the bunny body for a tail. Near the opposite end, help them glue on two 4-inch-long bunny ear shapes cut from white construction paper. Let the children use crayons or markers to draw on an eye and add pink shading to the ears. To complete the Bunny Puppets, glue or tape a craft-stick handle onto each one.

💡 Another Idea

Give each of your children a paper plate that has been folded in half and stapled closed around the edges. Let the children use the plates to make bunnies, as described in the main activity. Show them how they can manipulate their puppets by holding them in their hands.

Fingerprint Eggs

For each of your children, draw a simple basket shape on a piece of white or light-colored construction paper. Make paint pads by placing thin sponges in shallow containers and pouring on small amounts of different-colored tempera paint. Invite your children to press their fingers, one at a time, onto the paint pads and stamp fingerprint "eggs" all over their basket shapes.

 Another Idea

Hand out pieces of green construction paper. Let your children stamp colored fingerprints all over their papers to represent eggs in the grass. When the paint has dried, give them small amounts of green Easter grass to glue onto their pictures, if they wish.

Easter Egg Wall Decorations

From butcher paper, cut out an extra-large basket shape. Invite your children to sponge-paint pastel-colored designs onto the shape. Set out egg shapes cut from assorted colors of construction paper, along with collage materials, such as paper and fabric scraps, yarn, ribbon, rickrack, lace, and glitter glue. Let your children choose egg shapes and decorate them by gluing on the collage materials. When the glue has dried, attach the basket shape to a wall or a bulletin board and tape or glue on the decorated eggs.

Quick Tip

If you need more eggs for your large Easter basket, cut egg shapes out of colorful gift-wrap.

Another Idea

Invite your children to fingerpaint designs on construction paper or fingerprint paper. When the paint has dried, cut the papers into egg shapes and attach them to a green bulletin board border.

NEW! Early Learning Resources

For Teachers

Art Series

Great ideas for exploring art with children ages 3 to 6! Easy, inexpensive activities encourage enjoyable art experiences in a variety of ways.

Cooperative Art • Outdoor Art • Special Day Art

The Best of Totline—Bear Hugs

This new resource is a collection of some of Totline's best ideas for fostering positive behavior.

Celebrating Childhood Posters

Inspire parents, staff, and yourself with these endearing posters with poems by Jean Warren.

The Children's Song
Patterns
Pretending
Snowflake Splendor
The Heart of a Child
Live Like the Child
The Light of Childhood
A Balloon
The Gift of Rhyme

Circle Time Series

Teachers will discover quick, easy ideas to incorporate into their lessons when they gather children together for this important time of the day.

Introducing Concepts at Circle Time
Music and Dramatics at Circle Time
Storytime Ideas for Circle Time

Empowering Kids

This unique series tackles behavioral issues in typical Totline fashion—practical ideas for empowering young children with self-esteem and basic social skills.

Problem-Solving Kids
Can-Do Kids

Theme-A-Saurus

Two new theme books join this popular Totline series!

Transportation Theme-A-Saurus
Field Trip Theme-A-Saurus

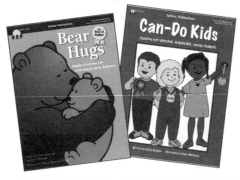

For Parents

My First Coloring Book Series

These coloring books are truly appropriate for toddlers—black backgrounds with white illustrations. That means no lines to cross and no-lose coloring fun! Bonus stickers included!

All About Colors
All About Numbers
Under the Sea
Over and Under
Party Animals
Tops and Bottoms

Happy Days

Seasonal fun with rhymes and songs, snack recipes, games, and arts and crafts.

Pumpkin Days • Turkey Days • Holly Days • Snowy Days

Little Builder Stacking Cards

Each game box includes 48 unique cards with different scenes printed on each side. Children can combine the cards that bend in the middle with the flat cards to form simple buildings or tall towers!

Castle
The Three Little Pigs

Rainy Day Fun

Turn rainy-day blahs into creative, learning fun! These creative Totline ideas turn a home into a jungle, post office, grocery store, and more!

Rhyme & Reason Sticker Workbooks

These age-appropriate workbooks combine language and thinking skills for a guaranteed fun learning experience. More than 100 stickers!

Up in Space • All About Weather • At the Zoo • On the Farm • Things That Go • Under the Sea

Theme Calendars

Weekly activity ideas in a nondated calendar for exploring the seasons with young children.

Toddler Theme Calendar
Preschool Theme Calendar
Kindergarten Theme Calendar

T☼tline® PUBLICATIONS

Teacher Resources

ART SERIES
Ideas for successful art experiences.
Cooperative Art
Special Day Art
Outdoor Art

BEST OF TOTLINE® SERIES
Totline's best ideas.
Best of Totline Newsletter
Best of Totline Bear Hugs
Best of Totline Parent Flyers

BUSY BEES SERIES
Seasonal ideas for twos and threes.
Fall • Winter • Spring • Summer

CELEBRATIONS SERIES
Early learning through celebrations.
Small World Celebrations
Special Day Celebrations
Great Big Holiday Celebrations
Celebrating Likes and Differences

CIRCLE TIME SERIES
Put the spotlight on circle time!
Introducing Concepts at Circle Time
Music and Dramatics at Circle Time
Storytime Ideas for Circle Time

EMPOWERING KIDS SERIES
Positive solutions to behavior issues.
Can-Do Kids
Problem-Solving Kids

EXPLORING SERIES
Versatile, hands-on learning.
Exploring Sand • Exploring Water

FOUR SEASONS
Active learning through the year.
Art • Math • Movement • Science

JUST RIGHT PATTERNS
8-page, reproducible pattern folders.
Valentine's Day • St. Patrick's Day •
Easter • Halloween • Thanksgiving •
Hanukkah • Christmas • Kwanzaa •
Spring • Summer • Autumn •
Winter • Air Transportation • Land
Transportation • Service Vehicles
• Water Transportation • Train
• Desert Life • Farm Life • Forest
Life • Ocean Life • Wetland Life
• Zoo Life • Prehistoric Life

KINDERSTATION SERIES
Learning centers for kindergarten.
Calculation Station
Communication Station
Creation Station
Investigation Station

1•2•3 SERIES
Open-ended learning.
Art • Blocks • Games • Colors •
Puppets • Reading & Writing •
Math • Science • Shapes

1001 SERIES
Super reference books.
1001 Teaching Props
1001 Teaching Tips
1001 Rhymes & Fingerplays

PIGGYBACK® SONG BOOKS
New lyrics sung to favorite tunes!
Piggyback Songs
More Piggyback Songs
Piggyback Songs for Infants
and Toddlers
Holiday Piggyback Songs
Animal Piggyback Songs
Piggyback Songs for School
Piggyback Songs to Sign
Spanish Piggyback Songs
More Piggyback Songs for School

PROJECT BOOK SERIES
*Reproducible, cross-curricular project
books and project ideas.*
Start With Art
Start With Science

REPRODUCIBLE RHYMES
*Make-and-take-home books for
emergent readers.*
Alphabet Rhymes • Object Rhymes

SNACKS SERIES
Nutrition combines with learning.
Super Snacks • Healthy Snacks •
Teaching Snacks • Multicultural Snacks

TERRIFIC TIPS
Handy resources with valuable ideas.
Terrific Tips for Directors
Terrific Tips for Toddler Teachers
Terrific Tips for Preschool Teachers

THEME-A-SAURUS® SERIES
Classroom-tested, instant themes.
Theme-A-Saurus
Theme-A-Saurus II
Toddler Theme-A-Saurus
Alphabet Theme-A-Saurus
Nursery Rhyme Theme-A-Saurus
Storytime Theme-A-Saurus
Multisensory Theme-A-Saurus
Transportation Theme-A-Saurus
Field Trip Theme-A-Saurus

TODDLER RESOURCES
Great for working with 18 mos–3 yrs.
Playtime Props for Toddlers
Toddler Art

Parent Resources

A YEAR OF FUN SERIES
Age-specific books for parenting.
Just for Babies • Just for Ones •
Just for Twos • Just for Threes •
Just for Fours • Just for Fives

LEARN WITH PIGGYBACK® SONGS
*Captivating music with
age-appropriate themes.*
Songs & Games for…
Babies • Toddlers • Threes • Fours
Sing a Song of…
Letters • Animals • Colors • Holidays
• Me • Nature • Numbers

LEARN WITH STICKERS
*Beginning workbook and first reader
with 100-plus stickers.*
Balloons • Birds • Bows • Bugs •
Butterflies • Buttons • Eggs • Flags •
Flowers • Hearts • Leaves • Mittens

MY FIRST COLORING BOOK
*White illustrations on black back-
grounds—perfect for toddlers!*
All About Colors
All About Numbers
Under the Sea
Over and Under
Party Animals
Tops and Bottoms

PLAY AND LEARN
Activities for learning through play.
Blocks • Instruments • Kitchen
Gadgets • Paper • Puppets • Puzzles

RAINY DAY FUN
*This activity book for parent-child fun
keeps minds active on rainy days!*

RHYME & REASON STICKER WORKBOOKS
*Sticker fun to boost
language development and
thinking skills.*
Up in Space
All About Weather
At the Zoo
On the Farm
Things That Go
Under the Sea

SEEDS FOR SUCCESS
*Ideas to help children develop
essential life skills for future success.*
Growing Creative Kids
Growing Happy Kids
Growing Responsible Kids
Growing Thinking Kids

Start right, start bright!

If you love Totline® books, you'll love

Totline® MAGAZINE

For Ages 2–5

Active Learning

Engage young children in hands-on learning that captivates their minds and imaginations.

Across the Curriculum

Each issue includes seasonal learning themes, open-ended art, songs and rhymes, language and science activities, healthy snack recipes, and more!

Proven ideas

We print ideas that work and time-tested tips submitted by professionals like yourself!

Especially for You

So you can do your job easier, we include reproducible parent pages, ready-made learning materials, special pull-outs, and ideas that are truly age-appropriate for preschoolers.

May/June 1999   Restaurants: A Giant Classroom Project $ 4.00

Totline
Active preschool learning at its best

The Fish Who Wished He Could Fly
by Jean Warren

Jump Into Spring
With Garden Games and Nature Crafts

Backyard Field Trips

Active preschool learning at its best!

SPECIAL! Group Subscription Rates

Activity calendar in each issue!